Cracked Around the Edges:

Selected Poems 2015-2019

Lily Maureen O'Nan

Cracked Around the Edges: Selected Poems 2015-2019

ISBN: 978-1-4583-2770-3

For Jessica, my love

Content

PART ONE: SURREALITY

(2015-2016)

Cracked Around the Edges

Orange fades grey.
Tomorrow will be another day.
Side-swashed,
And backwashed.
Like splintered crayon on the ground.
Flying, kaleidoscopic intrinsic,
Whereabouts.
The fly's nest is in,
The pond.
Without thoughtless,
Carelessness,
Or social reprieve.
Circumstantial obligations without,
Foundation.
Provides the masculine and feminine,
Within.
A means to navigate towards,
The Sun.
**

O'Nan

Swept up infinite currents of,
Matter and awareness.
Falling ever so sliding,
With timeless effervescence.
Triangular waves of consciousness.
Look a little on the sunny side,
As Ray Davies brings another,
Day.
Melody and full brass section.
Sliding back into rabbit,
Hole.
Holding Alice and squandering true liberty,
And flowing out like dusty shrines.
Smoldering that world.
Falling forward,
Ever so pleasantly.
Folding sing-song lullabies,
That forever dream.
I wonder if I am Bela Lugosi.
It's that time of year.
I am everyone and everything.
Sullenly implying left-wing politics,
To the rodeo pigs of,
Kentucky.
**

Cracked Around the Edges

Holding up stances that can save the,
Human race.
Vanishing vanished.
Breathing wind into broken robots.
Robust, with networking,
And status.
Trypta-know what I mean?
Forever lost in a glimpse of forever.
I found God in a mushroom.
**

O'Nan

Shedding light,
On past egos.
Forcing the shower of the spirit.
Forgetting tomorrow.
Becoming today.
Lifting the blindfold,
But without transcendence,
How can one see?
I faded,
And came back,
With intent,
To crawl forward.
Escaping the inevitable,
For just a moment in time.
Blessed to see the wishes,
Of others.
To sneak past the nightmares,
And become one,
With dismantled reality.
Forgiving just a trace,
Of the shadow.
To gain insight,
And stick there.
**

Cracked Around the Edges

Tiding the surface.
Raindrop enters brain,
Succeeding.
The seed brings forth virtue,
Like little elephant dodged,
Drafts of torrential downpour.
Exceeding limitation,
The right way.
Discovery fulfills fantasy,
With ringing bells,
Outside shattered glass.
Awaiting doorstep,
Of convenience.
Feeding the downpour now,
For the poor to eat and drink.
Finding the extravagance,
Too much, too soon.
Flight escapes freedom,
From triumph.
To be put together,
In someone else's,
Dream.
**

O'Nan

Healing in dealing,
With life's circumstances.
Lucid dances,
With dreaming faces,
Splattered against a facet,
Of reality,
Switched on and off.
Awareness begets consciousness.
Breeding the lack of,
Time.
Without time,
Inside and outside of clockwork.
Speechless,
But what are words,
But sound?
Sound the alarm.
Alarming, but,
You may never know,
How the wish may,
Unfold.
**

Cracked Around the Edges

Look into the morning,
Swinging forward.
Like depth and denial,
One does not exist in this state,
Alone.
Switching life on.
Flickering in industrial wayside.
Bringing the love.
Giving the love,
And moving,
Forward.
Lacking ability,
Yet a thriving machine,
Ingesting timeslots.
Intriguing guest work to solid,
Ground.
Exchanging swords with interdimensional,
Submarine dream.
Blanket out.
Back in,
Touch with,
Reality sliding.
Unusual framework of guilt,
That had built up.
Gone,
Like flame extinguishing,
Fire.
**

O'Nan

Dreams deny,
Existence to be,
Warm.
Seeing the outer,
Shell.
Inside the inner,
Workings.
Blame nothing.
See beyond,
And hear,
The sounds.
Scarred by fantasy,
But blooming scarcely,
And avoiding misery.
Breathe in,
To perceive.
Blind to all,
Is a greater,
Truth and connection.
**

Cracked Around the Edges

Nude like a parasitic,
Introspective,
Dreamwork.
Slinging the mud,
Outside the bright,
Morning.
Slimmed down,
To bone and breath.
Adrenaline rushes,
Through tears,
Melting slightly,
Like the horse you never,
Rode.
Time bewitches the,
Hour,
Forsaken to the charity,
That turns the tide.
Winding the clockwork,
Preservation.
**

O'Nan

Once upon a time,
I fell into the,
Gasping and heaving,
Of inside tranquilizing,
Shudders.
Tasting the voices,
Like moons and broo-ha-ha.
My moments,
Deceive.
My motives,
Incite,
The moments.
"But what is it worth?"
Said the momentary,
Lack of,
Motivation.
Motivated by a darkness,
Given light.
**

Cracked Around the Edges

Living part-time,
Divided.
Seemingly obvious is the nature,
Of existence.
Feed and die.
Live and thrive.
Fall asleep in,
Between,
Fallen branches.
Parasitic like a,
Raincoat,
Sludged against mirror.
Always falling,
For depth of breath.
Finalizing daydream.
Buckets of stale,
Feelings.
Slices of wedged and wet,
Time.
Fire feels the world,
Dividing once,
Again.
Winning the losing game,
With winter dying,
And only a spring of hope,
Arising.
**

O'Nan

Brain, brain, brain.
Mother,
Can you help me with the,
Rain,
Draining down?
Time has released,
The grime,
But,
The scene is so bleak,
And powerful.
The source is the,
Suggestion.
Sluggish reasoning,
Without,
Treason trying,
To fly.
The world,
What do you do,
Best?
I see the flame,
But I roar.
**

The Great Fall

Enhancing the traces.
Finding without falling,
Into the seams,
Of insanity.
Bringing back the carriage,
In anticipation,
Of goldless,
Transitions.
Figure on the right,
To the left.
Kind of like your mother.
Kind of like the sun,
Blaring.
Blurring the fluorescent,
Transcendence.
Arising outside,
The inner mind.
Blinking with totality,
And wisdom.
Maybe we all,
Fall short,
From time to time.
I am falling from the,
Inside,
But sliding along,
Once again.
**

O'Nan

Driven by the world,
To dream outside,
Reality.
Foreshadowing the greatness,
Of imagination.
Blinking inside brain,
Walks.
Exercises meant to,
Build strength.
The gossiping of,
Flower child,
Discriminates.
Wishing the favor were,
Spent,
And filtered.
Arise,
To bring joy,
To self.
Why do I sing,
So disjointed,
Like hurricane,
In grey wind?
You hurry so,
Carelessly.
Only to see,
The dying eye.
**

Cracked Around the Edges

Matter is what you make,
Of it.
Like a joke frowned upon,
The maze continues.
Sliding into the,
Sideways sidewalk.
Bridges don't burn,
Themselves.
See what I mean,
About superstition,
Young man?
I sweep past anything,
Devolving.
The solution is in the,
Tea.
Wild nights do not,
Forgive.
See the fortune teller,
Like a bank teller,
Telling the tale,
Of blues,
Without regard.
Trust never favors the,
Wicked.
**

O'Nan

Simplistic,
Is the nature,
Of life and,
Death.
To each their own,
But without attaching,
Your wings to the,
wall.
Windows show you the,
Mirror.
Riding along the,
Sunset daydream,
Evolved.
Plaguing the riddle,
With the many,
Words from,
Outside the,
Mainstream.
Bold is the spirit,
Finding itself,
To build strength.
Delivering the nuisance,
Of bewilderment,
Inside life's avoidance.
**

Cracked Around the Edges

Slight turn,
Of faith,
Blinded.
Bound together,
And pouring down,
Like sand,
Inside the outer realms,
Of castle life.
Bridging the gap.
Binging on tornadic,
Wind.
Wound down,
Inside hollow,
Ground.
Finding peace,
In darkness,
Forsaken.
Your plight,
Might,
Muddle the mind.
Too much,
Little time,
Mistaken for,
Identity.
Theft of the soul,
Branches out,
Like rays of sunshine.
**

O'Nan

Signing onto the,
Side of,
Transitioning.
I exist for,
The knowing of,
Planetary disturbances,
Faces the outside,
Of what you see.
Spider cider,
And rumpled tea.
Transformed,
Like rocket glares,
As I stare,
Into the moon clouds.
The lion lies,
Muddled in mud,
And angry at the wind.
For tomorrow I send,
My love,
Outward and in.
**

Cracked Around the Edges

Begging like,
Dogs inside,
Bone zones,
Filtered like webs.
The united fear,
The division,
Of splintered carriages.
Sitting in the fields,
Of inner tranquility.
The center of gravity,
Binds to the receptor.
My blind spot,
Is noticing the slight,
Turn of events.
Ranging from the fear,
To fantasy.
One grain of sand,
Can send me spiraling,
For your grasp,
Once again.
**

O'Nan

Wounded like a hurt dog,
Crying.
Talking behind my back.
The fleas eating me.
I've died before,
And I need true help.
**

Cracked Around the Edges

PART TWO: REALITY CHECK

2019

Cracked Around the Edges

Who gives a fuck,
If I just turn into dust?
Burn in the flames,
Cry if you must.
This world was not,
Made for me.
Bound to lie,
Into the sea of blood.
So sick and tired,
Of this façade,
That everyone thinks,
That I'm just a fraud.
What the fuck did I do,
To ask to be born?
I wish I could laugh,
But God knows I'm torn.
So fly away,
I don't care anymore.
So fly away,
I'm not here anyway.
**

O'Nan

Feeling rushed,
Must push to fight.
Grappling with anger and frustration,
It's mental masturbation.
So scared to ask for help,
Everyone ignores and avoids the problem.
These fuckers don't know shit,
About mental health,
Or how to help themselves.
No time to rest,
No time for self-care.
Compliance is my virtue,
Though I want to push back.
They leave me struggling,
For air,
I'm in deep despair.
This routine has broken me,
In two,
And my mind's a loose screw.
So fuck the discrimination,
Fuck the hate,
Kill off this white cishet bait,
And do your own thing,
Cause you'll make it out,
Alive and thrive.
**

Cracked Around the Edges

Pepper spray the mountaineer,
Straight in the face,
Have no fear.
What the fuck,
Is this beating heart?
Tear it out,
Floor's the door.
No one bleeds,
Like the kids bleed.
No one breeds,
Like the adult who leaves you,
crying.
**

O'Nan

This is insanity,
Don't cling to humanity.
I cried my tears,
Now say your prayers.
I'm tired of this,
Just make me new again.
I am terrified,
You all blow my mind.
What do you want?
What do you need?
Can you tell me, please?
I plead for you.
I never would have left you two.
But you left me,
Sobbing,
And wishing I was dead.
Fuck you too,
For thinking you ever loved,
Me.
I gave you insurance, doctor,
Therapy.
But you blocked all that out,
Because you no longer wanted me.
So goodbye and good riddance,
At the same time.
**

Cracked Around the Edges

Five million ghosts,
Ride the dead sea,
Wide open,
Inside of me.
I collide indifferently,
To five million ghosts,
Bleeding deep wounds,
To start day from day.
I'm sorry that I'm here,
To be a lonely dried up,
Queer.
Building up the world,
To be brought down to tears.
I'm scared of the roadblocks.
Afraid of this scene.
All of this deepness,
Collides over me,
And at once,
No peace to be.
**

O'Nan

Stomach supplies the system,
As energy is fuel.
Don't sigh too deeply,
Or things become creepy.
I am trying,
To fix this broken,
System.
Don't close off reality,
For what is supposed to be.
Look within,
Then seek without.
You are your own pathway,
To communication.
Reach out to others,
To find what is within.
The mind may play tricks,
But there is much to fix.
Do not doubt,
That you can accomplish,
Without delay,
The matters that sprout,
Injustice and destruction,
From living in debt,
Default to conclusion.
**

Cracked Around the Edges

The wetness feels the heat,
Mapping the weather of the sleet.
All bleak and bloody,
Love.
I want to rise above,
The groaning missing piece.
We are two cats in heat,
Blind to the hatred of one,
Another.
Send me a valentine,
And I will cry for more.
No focus to describe,
This dining of the whore.
Moonlight to sunrise,
We send signals from inside.
Raising our brows,
Like werewolves set to teeth.
Breathing in the lies,
That once could set us free.
And so we die,
Together.
Put me to rest,
To lie in a peaceful nest,
Of longing to deny,
The prettiness inside.
**

O'Nan

The dream is complete,
To lie here in the street.
Minding my own business,
Has never been inquisitive.
Tomorrow may not tell,
But today is a ringing bell.
Shine now in the timeless,
Utterly crying nightless,
Wishes.
Time is insensitive,
To the world's demanding,
Richness.
So die away the leaves,
That fall among the deeds,
Of yesterday's harvest,
Falling, but starlit.
Sickness builds a world,
To swirl, and fall, and drool.
Acid daydreams escape,
The in-built rape,
Of a million falling meteors,
Flying from the sun,
To create the beauty,
We all find outside,
Ourselves.
**

Cracked Around the Edges

Glue filling the muddy,
Blood.
Sealing the deal,
The final meal.
Building blocks of,
Mildewed brains.
Dry the wind,
I have no skin,
To seep into,
I suppose I can't marry you.
The death has risen,
Between us,
And there is no way,
To unite us someday.
You broke our promise,
Now fade and grimace.
Blind hatred feeds,
The soulless demon,
In me.
But echoes fade,
I am but gray.
No black and white,
Just appetite,
Now feed the wine,
To the morning sunshine.
**

O'Nan

The leakage complete,
A blindly wrecking heat.
The wind blows heavily here,
Upon spaced-out, slightly crooked,
Queer.
Vision explodes,
Outside auditory textbook,
Sensory over time.
Time expands like,
Demons flying slowly,
On top of the sliding scale,
Of doubt.
Seize the means,
Of seduction.
The binary is destruction,
Of the will.
**

I Live Outside My Body

The remembrance,
Of things unknown,
To others.
I live outside,
My body.
I breathe in the tobacco,
Smoke,
With passion.
My only escapism,
Is music, writing, and smoking,
Yet it all brings me back,
To my emotions.
Sometimes I want to cry,
About the destruction,
Of earth.
I feel sad,
That all living beings die,
To their original source,
Because they are no longer,
With us.
All we can do is,
Try to survive,
This damage.
I wish I had,
A better answer,
But I'm slowly working on it.
**

O'Nan

The house pours,
Out your brain,
Like a severed puzzle,
Of broken wishes.
I will fly above you,
But it is only,
Disconnection,
Holding me together.
It seems that the world,
Is discolored slightly,
But we are in debt,
To the falcon of death.
Do you read me?
Can you read me?
There are too many,
Left to suffer against,
Noisy backgrounds,
Incessant.
Living is no longer,
A nightmare,
When I see your face.
It is like pacing,
Back and forth,
In contentment.
Let us,
Freeze together.
**

Cracked Around the Edges

The doctor won't,
Give me a shot,
To save my life.
Why?
Can't you smile for,
Once,
Or does it bother you,
That I care,
About your wellbeing?
I am waiting for a time,
To unite,
And breathe the same,
Breath.
We shall save each other,
From detriment.
No more discreet,
Affiliation.
The heteros will then be,
A wreck,
And we will take over,
Our own domain.
Love is a resonance,
Of longing,
To be forever,
Together,
Drifting in the same lane.
**

O'Nan

I wish I could kiss,
Jesus,
As she flies,
Like butterfly,
To sky.
You are the lead,
Diamond,
Shining beyond,
Control,
Of shimmy and seizure.
I shall recant,
That your position,
Is imaginary,
A façade,
A fake face.
Just like you were a,
False friend.
I peel the layers off,
Behind your brain.
You have just bought,
The one-way ticket,
To hell.
Let's get help,
As if anyone's opinion,
Matters anyway.
**

Cracked Around the Edges

Limb after limb,
You climb the heart.
Tell me what you are,
Looking for,
Artistic advice or,
Autistic advice?
I will give you both,
From the top of brain.
You shall also receive it,
From the deepness of,
My soul.
The world twirls,
As men drool,
Down the path not taken,
For generosity.
Incomplete and stagnant,
At times,
But you speak the truth,
So eloquently,
And beautifully.
Sing to me,
In a broken language,
And I will jump for joy,
That you spoke,
Only for me.
**

O'Nan

A glass of wine,
Won't last all night.
Hell, take the whole bottle,
Take two.
And yet,
Here I am,
The opposite of wasted.
However, as I type words,
They look completely foreign.
I think this gives,
The wrong impression.
But why impress,
This person,
In particular?
Nothing can be said,
By moonlight,
Apparently.
So, I just jot down the words,
Because everything,
Figures itself out,
Somehow.
Language is powerful,
When one can,
Decipher it.
**

Cracked Around the Edges

The smoke of this cigarette,
Makes my mind feel,
Organized.
But once in a while,
It feels disconnected,
Unbuttoned,
And re-conditioning itself,
In the worst sense possible.
My stomach is empty.
I need calories to,
Survive,
But I have been sitting for hours,
At trauma's front door.
I miss the way,
The petals hit your face,
In a strange reverie,
In between,
You and me.
This night glows onward,
And I don't want this to be,
A repeated cycle.
Dopaminergic,
But not so unplastered,
I fill shapes with gold,
To complete the disaster.
**

O'Nan

This life tends,
To show us glimpses,
Of Hell at these,
Late hours.
It has gotten past,
The point of,
Sleep.
Is this implied,
Insanity?
Is this what my consciousness,
Has become,
But I believe I will,
Eventually,
Get to a point where,
My functioning improves.
These hours are,
Very cruel,
To the psyche.
Maybe just focus,
On the love we share.
You know,
I believe you can improve,
My life,
But I know,
It takes time.
**

Cracked Around the Edges

This feeling,
Is incorrect,
And a disconnection.
Notice every single,
Hair,
On your body,
Just wishing you had,
Motivation.
We call this,
Dysphoria,
All wrong.
Genitals should die out,
Through evolution,
Or make me the way,
I wish to be.
**

O'Nan

I can feel the needle,
Creeping in.
My emotions become,
Empty,
At night.
I soar through the sky,
Like a desperate raven,
Trying to feed on a,
Rock.
There are dysfunctions,
That take over,
Like brain on bread.
Is this what life,
Has to be,
Or was I one of the,
Lucky ones?
Enduring everything,
At maximum,
Feeds my wounds well.
Have you ever sunk,
So low,
That you would live,
In a beat up,
Brick,
Sanctuary?
**

Peepshow

There is a peepshow,
That sells attitudes,
Of anguish.
You may very well be,
Self-taught,
In your motivations,
But the brain is fucked,
Together like ice.
We bleed together,
And sing party songs.
The feeling is,
Monstrous,
Like parasite on dead wind.
**

O'Nan

You can't take from me,
What you already have.
There is no stop,
To going mad.
Shrinky dink,
I see nothing of benefit,
But myself.
You didn't unite me,
You simply made me the enemy,
Of myself.
Persecute your own bitch,
Because I'm not the snitch.
You publicized my despair,
For your own political affair.
Fuck off with your so-called,
Revolution solution,
It's just an illusion.
This system is not repairing,
Me,
And I feel endangered.
Doxx your fucking grandma,
Cheap thief,
Lack of sleep.
I am not obligated to conform,
To your "master plan,"
Fucking cheap ass labor,
To stake your claim of reality.
You stole my mind,
Now give it back.
As soon as possible,
Eat the rich,
No difference.
Go live your own,
Fucked up delusion.
**

Cracked Around the Edges

This is not reality,
The trust I had in you,
Went to shit,
And you can call it a fit.
But it's my brain,
You're playing with.
I don't need your,
Office chair officers.
You corrupt media,
For pleasure.
There is no preciousness,
In your pretty,
Messed up head.
It's all part of their,
Experiment.
"They, they, they."
It's them.
We don't have to comply,
To civil demands,
We can rally in our hearts.
Feel the goddamn,
Rumbling of egg,
Snatched from purity.
All the time you invest in me,
Could be better spent,
Eating peanut butter by,
The spoonful for weeks.
I don't have to be dehumanized,
By computerized associations.
You brought the enemy,
To me and now,
I demand a,
Recall.
**

O'Nan

The wish is in the hand,
Of palm reader sublime.
Sending feedback loops,
Backwards to forward,
Extinction of species.
We will not see the limit,
Until we cement ourselves,
Into cradled universe.
Expansion of the scope,
Otherwise unfulfilled.
Let's bully the insanity,
Of nature's existence.
With sand gleaning the,
Silence on repeat,
Lingering ever obstructed,
By terra cotta memory,
Self-illusion.
Just throw in the,
Vengeance to sever,
The light of day.
The sight of the,
Death of birth sits quietly,
In mind,
At all times.
You must salvage what,
You have left,
And not give in to the,
Persuasion of brain tremors,
Affecting the life.
There is an attainment,
Of universe,
In others,
Sent to help transform,
You.
**

Cracked Around the Edges

Solitary sadness in midriff,
Slighted toward ridiculous,
Questioning of feeling,
Hurt.
Really want to cry,
As this reconnection,
From conditioned brainwashing,
Truly feels isolating.
I am unsure how to,
Express the falling,
Of fading.
Sensation guilts pain,
Of love for too much,
Time.
Broken as one is,
There are all of these,
Pieces that are connecting,
And disconnecting.
My heart breaks every night,
And then comes desolate,
Communication.
At least I can feel still,
As I had wondered,
If that component was gone.
Please cry,
I plea for tears,
Please.
Why the fuck am I so,
Hopeless now?
This mental discrepancy,
Of thought versus emotion,
Is desperate,
To cry.
**

Jess & Lily (Re-sought)

It took dying to remember,
Your embrace,
To teach me less,
About the ways the liar kills.
The truth is ever eminent,
Soaking in my breast,
The laughter, the tears,
And all the rest.
I need your love,
As you need me.
We will be with us,
Forever free to be.
The time is right,
And I feel so that,
We don't have to fight,
The nature of who we are.
Everything creates itself,
And we return back,
To ourselves,
As one.
Unite, we see,
The light to be,
Free to be,
Our lives for thee.
Impression had haunted,
Me.
Broke down,
Cigarettes and waking up,
On the ground.
And now the pieces,
Shall fix and connect,
What was always meant,
To be.
Us.
**

Cracked Around the Edges

There is no difference,
Between,
The ground and,
The sky.
No recollection,
Conceived of a mighty,
Sigh.
Bemoaning protrusion,
Like singing in,
Pain.
No time to,
Be,
A rainy,
Day.
Such timeless collecting,
Of fear in disguise.
Disgust the lesion,
Serenade the day.
The only way,
Of Middle Earth.
**

O'Nan

Slowly eliminating,
The desperate,
Pain.
As if the morning,
Is always a,
Winter's day.
No snow but,
Confusion.
Timeless transition.
Regenderated.
In time,
Immemorial.
Forever to stay,
At peace with,
One.
And Venus so caring,
Her Lily is,
Here to stay.
**

About the Author

Lily Maureen O'Nan is a multiply neurodivergent, queer nonbinary student at the University of Southern Indiana, studying psychology and working towards an associate degree in social science. They are planning to then move on to a bachelor's degree in psychology and sociology with a minor in gender studies. As a nonbinary transfeminine individual, they chose to publish these works to highlight the transformation that took place between the time of 2015-2019. They advocate for disability rights and hope to one day be able to write more about psychology, sociology, neurodiversity studies, queer theory, fiction, as well as more poetry.